THE WILD ROSES RUN

Douglas Richardson

Also by Douglas Richardson

<u>Fiction</u>

American Strays, featuring:
The Corruption of Zachary R.
Trust Fund Baby
Kay Sutter Through the Ages

<u>Poetry</u>

The Book of Good Dreams
Ghosts in Time and Space
Poems for Loners
Out in the Cold, Cold Day
Sugar Fish

THE WILD ROSES RUN

Douglas Richardson

Weak Creature Press
Los Angeles

The Wild Roses Run
©2017 by Douglas Richardson
Weak Creature Press

This is a work of poetry and fiction. Any resemblance to actual persons, living or deceased, events, or locations is entirely coincidental.

ISBN: 978-0-9842424-0-5

Printed in the United States of America.

Cover design by Heather DeSerio, Precision Edge Design LLC.

Author photo by Prudence Smuggery.

Contents

For Jen

Madrigal, Madrigal

Madrigal, madrigal
The many voices come
And from the graves
Upon the earth
The wild roses run

The Street-Art Oil Painting

The street-art oil painting
From Venice, California
Contained a hidden image meant just for him,
Told him he was a chosen one
From the western wall of his studio apartment,
Seduced him,
Said he belonged among philosopher kings
Or rock stars on late-night talk shows,
Then turned on him,
Got him mocked in pretentious bars,
Erased good, simple memories
Like the morning newspaper
On the porch of his childhood home;
So he shredded it with a box cutter
And scattered it across the street
With the neighbors watching.
Now he has humility, notoriety,
A wizard's beard that whistles in the dark.

MIB

Men in black beanies sit in a Jack in the Box
where no one over the age of forty
has ever smiled. Ask them whether
the moon is new or full and they couldn't say
because the sky no longer captivates them,
or perhaps it does hold them captive
and so the light they see might as well be
the light in this room: cool, even, anemic.
Moody devils, lonesome beauties,
if only I could lead them out the door
and into their ideal worlds.

Twenty-Two Centuries Ago

Twenty-two centuries ago
When the sky was green
The sun was gray
The moon was purple
And time went backwards

When America was in the south
Australia was in the north
Kangaroos could talk
Crocodiles could dance
And butterflies lived for 700 years

The aliens came down and said
"Please, please, press our button"
And because you did
Everything is how it is now

On the Roof

On the roof a Frisbee that doubled
as a flying saucer
a tennis ball the color of the moon
a doll with angelic eyes

Kids play
in the street below
like they don't even miss them

Like they've already forgotten about looking up

Hale-Bopp Cult

They set off together by lying down under purple
cloth and taking poison; purple because they knew
that black awaited them: that black we all prefer
not to think about. Still, this was better than their
terrestrial circumstances, still better than
San Diego.

Then, beyond all honest expectation, the plan
worked: purple-caped in absolute zero, a troupe of
immortals, still together, not wishing to return or
needing to, not accompanied by aliens, as they
thought, but an inkling of well-being, a barely
perceptible fraternal joy, what they had in
San Diego.

The History of Western Civilization

He learned the British names and ancestry
of her stuffed animals and spoke with them every
day, even when she wasn't there.

She kept a manila folder filled with recipes from
Greece and Italy and made a new dish every week,
even though she hated garlic.

It bore fruit until its 2075th birthday,
even though it was haunted by wanderlust
and whose Christ was a rose it would never see:

What an olive tree did for a Corsican village
A woman for her future husband
A man for his future wife

Another Sunday's Scattered Clouds

Another Sunday's scattered clouds
and fifty miles to the Lancaster poppy fields—
the poppies are not in bloom, but
the poppies are not the reason.
Driving into the high desert is the reason
listening to music is the reason
and afterward sitting with black coffee
and a maple bar in a Palmdale doughnut shop
where I can be alone with my ghost
for two or even three hours
and the doughnut lady won't say a thing because
she has a day of the week
and a place of asylum just like me.

Desert Rose

She removes the left shoe,
the hospital wristband,
the right shoe with the shoestrings frayed,
then she wanders after dark
still looking for the shade

Haight-Ashbury

The menacing dance of a tweaker, his head
swinging with the weight of a wrecking ball,
his eyes in waking REM,
each with a dream of its own.

A house for sale on Central Avenue,
cold as a clawfoot bathtub, complete with
hovering flies and a portrait of a chimpanzee
drawn in crayon by a sixty-year-old.

Biker's Lament

The leather-vested biker
in the devil dog bar
spilled his beer across the pool table
and cried over the forty years of clothes
he's seen scattered on the roadside

A Year in Leaves and Coins

Leaves debuted in greens
and exited in browns
boring all the eyes
of middle-aged clowns

Coins multiplied and glimmered
at the bottoms of fountains
fleeting desires
in evening gowns

Mean and Nice

I'd like to roll Wes Anderson's
windows down, so the bees can fly
in and around

I'd like to give Van Gogh
an audio tour
of the Musée d'Orsay

I'd like to thank Ed Ruscha
for undiscovering the country

I'd like to sit with Lady Di
and watch *Amélie*

She's Taking Ecstasy

She's taking ecstasy and
  Pushing ice
    Along a stranger's spine

The morning comes with spikes
  And suspect images
    In her mind:

A peacoat nightmare, a handbag
  Lost on god-knows-where stairs,
    A million lanterns on Broadway

Today is a sick day
  An omelet and hash browns day
    In a Divisadero diner
      With insomniac eyes, then

An afternoon alone:
  A Tom Collins on the windowsill
    Of the light well:

The shady light well, the
  Tranquil light well, a cabinet
    With the right pharmaceuticals

The Light Wells of San Francisco

Somewhere on Sansome

Apartment Six

Summer is cold
  Summer is cold
    In San Francisco
      Summer is cold

Set the Marlboro Lights
  In the light well
    Because
      The package is
        Pale gold . . .

The light wells of
  San Francisco are
    Intimate empty spaces
      Where only eyes may go
      And the neighbors
        Leave only traces:

Consider the woman
  In apartment twenty,
    One of 4,033
      Self-styled

Fag hags
   In the county

She set a red-leafed
  Poinsettia
   In the light well
    In August—is that
     Appropriate in August?

People on the streets
  Wear scarves in August,
   Which makes them difficult
   To see, suffocating in
    Scarved melancholy or

Winding along like snakes
  From one of seventeen
  San Francisco gates
  To the underworld

Dear God, please come into
  My heart and forgive me of
  All my sins; I seem to be
  Gaining you, but I'm
   Losing all my friends:

Consider the family in
  Apartment thirty,
   Won't let their kids

In the light well
Because

It's damp and grimy.
They gaze at me
With tenderness,
Which comes across
As pity

Or the man in
Apartment fourteen, who
Slams down his window
On account of my smoking

I see him in the hallway
With his girls and their asses;
He says I'm the one with the
Asshole glasses on the
Bridge of my nose. I'd like

To blow smoke in his face,
But what would you propose?

Apartment Twenty

Dear smoker in
Apartment six:

Can you do that thing
   Where you make your
      Eyes go dead?

Do you imagine a massacre
   In your head or just me
      Moving out of the neighborhood
         Once and for all?

I know you don't care
   For my male friends with
      Their stray-cat physiques

Or my red poinsettia
   In the light well

I owe you no explanation
   I have nothing to sell
      But no one wants
         To see you suffer

Apartment Thirty

Mama and Papa passed the bar exam
   And our FICO scores are on the mend
      Soon we'll be able to send our baby sharks
         To school in Tiburon, where,

18

Someday, we'll look across the Bay
　And quiver at the thought of
　　The sick nicotine sheen
　　　In the light well on Sansome

The psychotic soul in apartment six—
　Does he still mutter to God? Did he
　　Think we couldn't hear him?
　　　How humiliating

Apartment Fourteen

The seminarian in number six
　Hates my jeans and rattail braid
　　Wonders why he can't get laid
　　　In those asshole red-framed glasses

Poinsettia lady in twenty
　Could tell him why, but he
　　Doesn't have the guts to listen

He glares at my girlfriends
　Because he doesn't really want them
　　Then he smokes up the light well
　　　Like a chimney

Apartment Six

Summer is cold
  Summer is cold
    In San Francisco
      Summer is cold

Set the Marlboro Lights
  In the light well
    Because
      The package is
        Pale gold . . .

Outside the Last Bookstore

The homeless dance like Saint Vitus at
5th and Spring, like

the word "rude" spelled backward
signifying everything

The ambulance on the sidewalk
is for the laughing man coughing

The buildings remain stone through it all

Young Americans Find Freedom

Young Americans find freedom in
abandoned desert motels, chain-link fences
peeled back, fast-food wrappers swirling
in the dirt

Who cares if they're doing drugs?
I hope they're joking about
the paper strip across the toilet
like it won a beauty pageant
and the bath mat that says
"Welcome to Western Vacationland"
with water-skiers from the 1950s

I hope they're laughing like kaleidoscopes
and dreaming filthy dreams
among the snakes and roaches

Kincardine by the Freeway

Kincardine sounds like a purple blossom that grows
on a vine, but it's not. It's a street by the freeway
near a car wash and an establishment called Skin.

Skin is referred to as a gentlemen's club, but it's
not. Skin is where strippers shake it for money.

Strippers say the money is to put their children
through medical school, but it's not.

There are no children, just strippers spinning
around poles in a bar called Skin, while I'm thinking
about vines of Kincardine.

Littlerock, California

The child went to school for a time until a pack of dogs kept her off the streets for good. The owner insisted they were harmless until the neighbor lady was mauled to death. The boy's in prison now, but a dog or two still roam wild. So the child stayed inside listening to desert sand blast against the cinder blocks, and that sound diminished by the Doritos crunching inside her skull. She only began noticing these sounds after the TV broke and she pretended to care for the sake of her mom, who worries so much about her, about how her daughter's apathy costs her. The child hated the TV, the vanity of it. What reason could anyone possibly have to be so vain? A year ago she hitched a ride on the Pearblossom Highway. Today she saw her name, photo, date of birth, height, weight, etc., on a perforated strip beneath a Domino's Pizza coupon. Her roommate joked that she was famous now to anyone with a mailbox in Los Angeles County. "You're not 180 pounds, though," said her roommate. "Sure I am," said the child, not wanting to call her mom but dialing the number anyway.

Everybody Likes Stevie Wonder

It was the burnt-orange year 1976 when my dad and I entered Canoga Park to purchase a metal desk to stack his *Motor Trend*s on.

I was irritating him and myself with my frequent changing of radio stations and so decided to leave it on the next station no matter what song came on. It was that Stevie Wonder song that sounds like a sparkly red beanbag that sticks to your legs when you try to stand up.

My dad bobbed his head to the song, so I didn't dare change the station again.

A neighbor kid once said that Stevie Wonder put his mouth right up to the mic when he sang, and that's why he was so good. The neighbor kid gave a visual demonstration by placing his fist (the microphone) against his lips. Everyone there nodded in agreement. I felt light-headed and had to sit down on the curb. Everyone there looked at me suspiciously.

My dad stopped bobbing his head and turned off the radio before the song ended because we had pulled into the parking lot of the furniture warehouse. My dad and the warehouse salesman laughed and barked and banged the metal desks around until one was chosen. After my dad signed the paperwork, the salesman offered me a Tootsie Pop. I took it and immediately looked down at the cracked cement floor to avoid his eyes. My dad looked amused and vaguely disgusted. I mean everybody likes Stevie Wonder.

All the Cylinder-Shaped Holiday Inns

All the cylinder-shaped Holiday Inns along the
freeway—the sky, of course, is gray in that I-have-
to-drive-to-Oxnard-to-buy-some-tires kind of way
and the windshield wipers are set to intermittent
but they're really not needed so the rubber
screeches on the glass.

Our youth soccer days are gone, our dreams
mitigated, and so long to them for they were silly,
like a 16-year-old in a copper-colored Kia Soul
driving eighty down Bolsa Chica in Westminster
trying to get to Surf City USA but winding up
at the Army Recruiting Center in the strip mall
instead.

Kell

Kell is released
by
the high school bell.

She boards a
40-year-old bus
that idles
while the traffic lights
            one-two-three.

Then it's
up
the on-ramp
past a smoke-blackened mural
that she hasn't noticed
since
middle school.

Hobo

A field of straw a foot high in the summer dirt
the heat of the day lingers here
in the windless twilight of a seaside town
of tents and newsprint
across the field all the lights of a
traveling carnival come to rest
all the moving lights
and what must be smoke
though it tastes like dust
and I know nobody there
and no one knows I'm here

Weeks He Holds

Weeks he holds a steady job
Weekends are for long walks, muttering

Years pile up
And years pile on, then

His stretch of sidewalk clears

Up above, the water turns white
And eventually disappears

He Sat Outside

He sat outside in his hospital gown
tossing almond shavings
to a trusting blackbird.

He was a trustworthy man
who didn't mind iron chairs
or his hands touching the sidewalk.

His eyes swept wide as an alluvial fan
accepting the full spectrum of light.

Soon a chain of blackbirds arrived
at his feet.

Your Resurrection

Your resurrection is complete
The vultures lie dead at your feet
In an otherwise empty field
So now what?
Are you still the same person
Dying to make a million?
Are you still the same frivolous Roman?
Or will you sit in a tree and strum a guitar?
Or hide in a library and plot against a tyrant?
Will you protest, demonstrate, crusade?
Be the savior and the saved?
Play the mensch and invite an enemy
For coffee?
And don't trouble yourself about those birds
Their energy was conserved, and whatever
They're doing now beats pecking
At the eyes of their fellow creatures

The Birds Will Sing and the Holy Ghost Will Visit

1.
The birds will sing no matter what I'm thinking
whether it's how a flagpole in the wind
sounds like church bells on Easter
or how I wasted a year trying to even a score
the birds will sing forevermore

2.
The Holy Ghost will visit from time to time
I've got two words for that: sublime sublime

Heard but Not Seen

Distant trains and mission bells have caused
generations of philosophers to wander off into the
hills to wonder among the buzzing insects, their
troubled thoughts producing a scent like anise.

My Artist Friends

Oscar behaves like a pouty ballerina
his girlfriend chops kale on Formica
convinced that adulthood has little to impart
he enters his toy room and makes pediatric art
his glasswork brightens hospitals worldwide

Joanne is a lawyer, has a boa constrictor
called Sawyer who chases mice around a terrarium;
serpent-eyed and rich
her insomnia's a bitch
she'll paint dystopian cityscapes when she's retired

Mike is adrift in the auto-part desert
he appreciates the Del Taco aesthetic
he drives alone on Mojave highways
taking photos with his eyes
the purple in his sunsets is astounding

Lorelei loves elephants and monkeys and France
rococo tapestries put her in a trance
she colors her hair and takes the children
to the zoo
she believes in hair dye
the children believe too

Calabasas Girls

Calabasas girls make baubles for Buddha
sell them at the farmers market

they see no contradiction in competitive yoga
make fun of philosophers wearing togas

turquoise bangles
orange bangles
got balls in their pants
like Mr. Bojangles

poison their faces to relax their wrinkles
sneak a cupcake with infinite sprinkles

Llewellyn, Llewellyn

Llewellyn, Llewellyn, go back to hell,
where the old bats in the Roosevelt Hotel
feed on your tales of Hollywood stardom
and their hair falls out
from the heavy metal poisoning.

Llewellyn, Llewellyn,
the god of mercy wanted to make things right,
put us in the supermarket that night;
but you could never resist the cheap shot,
and how your head did swell.

Llewellyn, Llewellyn, go back to hell,
your toxic candy has made me ill;
feed it to the old bats in the Roosevelt Hotel;
they seem to think it's vitamins.

Twins

Twin garbage trucks
block the street
every Monday
at 6 a.m.

"788" stenciled on the back of the one
"789" on the back of the other

Sure, everyone hates them now
but they were once
somebody's
newborn babies

I Ate Lunch

I ate lunch with Andy Warhol

His hair stayed right in place

Then the bugs moved it an inch

Which put a stinger in my forehead

Bare Mattress

the sheet
is torn
down by
his feet

he can
feel the
bare mattress
there

it burns
a little
more
when the
bugs
scurry up
his shinbone

A Man Lies Aging

A man lies aging
in his bed

his toe is black
it's going dead

but
night air
comes through
the open window, cools
his face and lungs

and
clouds go by
quiet and low
lit from below
by the city lights

Pharaoh Touched the Treetops

Pharaoh touched the treetops in the evening,
saw the lights in the hills
and the mountains beyond the hills,
the freeways twisting and turning
and straightening out,
leading the way home for everyone who placed
a magnificent stone in the pyramid

Beginnings

People sit in crowded restaurants
pretending they don't hear the song
but nine years later
alone in a drive-thru
they'll hear it again
and let it all go
right there in the car
they'll let it all go

I Hear Music

I hear music but I can't tell where it's coming from
somewhere in the near distance most likely
(a courtyard or open window)
but it sounds far away
from another time and place
echoing off walls
and
into my ears

All the Old Bachelors

All the old bachelors
Sit in Subway restaurants
Listening to Adele set fire to the rain

The house cats of Laurel Canyon do the same
Because their rooms are damp
With spinsters in pain

Acquaintances of a Day

I could be talking about the weather,
a snail crossing a sidewalk in the rain;

or
a point of light in the sky at night,
the feeling of goodwill it produces;

or
faces contorting on the ceiling in the morning,
not one pleasing, not one wishing me good day;

or
a woman on a bus dying to scream and cuss,
the earnest line of her mouth refusing;

or
a lizard on a wall posing for antiquity;

or
any passerby, really

Multitudes Battle

Half are wounded
Half are dead
Clouds pass gently overhead

Santa Monica Revival

1.
There's a Ferris wheel spinnin' on the pier,
on the pier,
and the waves, they're a-spinnin' down below;
there's a Ferris wheel spinnin' on the pier,
on the pier,
and the waves in the water down below.

There's a man, he's a-watchin' on the bluff,
on the bluff,
there's a man, he's a-watchin' on the bluff;
there's a reed, it's a-growin' on the bluff,
on the bluff,
there's a reed turnin' green on the bluff.

And I don't know if I get it, but I do it,
but I do it,
don't know if I get it, but I do it;
there's a Ferris wheel spinnin' on the pier,
on the pier,
and the waves, they're a-spinnin' down below.

2.
I was sufferin' in the bus stop stench
I was waitin' on the mourners' bench
now I'm rollin' down the road
with the heat waves risin'
rollin' down the road
with the heat waves risin'

Decades

Summer rain fell on the ancient ruins.

I was alive in the archeology.

The traveler thought he recognized me.
I wanted to feel like that.

Religious gatherings
brought me closer to the others,
but I had to be alone
to hold onto it.

In the mountains I saw the pine trees
and the lake.

Jet planes flew over the valley.
There were no people below.

All my dreams combined
made the icy tail of a comet.

Hope

It arrived whole and slowly faded
yet, in fading, it ripened:

Like the song I didn't want to forget
so I drove for miles in silence

Like the colors of a Ferris wheel
in a black-and-white photo

Like the city so ideal
I had to close my eyes to see it

Like the fountain in the center
of the courtyard

Bishop, California

I'd like to be in Bishop, California
In the eastern Sierra Nevada
In the aisles of a hardware store
In the season of blue jeans and flannel
Buying tools for home improvement
Turning a nickel for a gumball
On my way out the door

I'd like to be in a booth in a diner
Looking at the snowy mountains
My fingers through the ear of a cup of coffee
Green pines, hot breakfast, close family
Living the life of a builder and a fixer
New wrenches in the back of my truck
And not a thief for miles around

Death Is the Best Adventure:

First you're handed a gift card that says
Your Money Is No Good Here, then
You're alone in a hotel room
With a Bible in a drawer

That doesn't sound so good anymore
But the Bible is a coast-to-coast trucker
Listening to the radio
And watching the scenery go by
Says you were Grant and he was Lee
Or was it the other way around
He can't remember

Death is the best adventure:
A chance to hear Louis Armstrong and Gabriel
Play a passage for trumpet
An opportunity to meet Anne Frank
And all her friends

Whatever you desire awaits you there;
And you can go now, but we still want you here

Walking in the Museum

Walking in the museum not thinking about death
Not lacking inspiration
Not feeling bereft
This isn't usually the way it goes
In every room flirtatious
In no room morose
It's because in the sculpture garden
I saw a ladder that twisted into the sky
And I saw where we'll all be by and by

The Last Friend

You knew when it was the last friend you had.
You knew when there wouldn't be another.
Now there's a plant under a staircase
that's thirsty for water.
Now there's a plant under a staircase
that you water.

The days are spent sleeping,
the nights drifting with the river,
where the mud lies so heavy
you can feel your arms hanging.

And you remember the day when there was no
more use for working.

And you don't think about a child, even where
there are children.

And your hands in your pockets bring memories of
warm kitchens and smiles coming down from the
ceiling.

Now cars after cars go under bridges where you're
walking. You don't stop because there's sadness in
looking.

You don't stop till the vast grasses and wild roses are running, and you don't care what you look like anymore. You don't know what you look like anymore.

The Green Bug

The green bug on my window screen
flew out into the rain

I know there are millions just like it
but I'll never see that one again

Acknowledgments

Special thanks to my editors, Jen Richardson, Laura Popelka, and Greg Dalgleish, for their expert guidance in the evolution and completion of this book.

Thanks also to *Poetry Super Highway* for publishing "Mean and Nice," "The Street-Art Oil Painting," "Bishop, California," and "MIB."

About the Author

Douglas Richardson was born on February 20, 1967, in Duluth, Minnesota, and was raised in Camarillo, California. He currently lives in Los Angeles with his wife, Jen.